Cleopatra

Katie Daynes

Illustrated by Serena Riglietti

History consultant: Dr. Anne Millard

Series editor: Lesley Sims

Designed by Russell Punter and
Katarina Dragoslavic

First published in 2004 by Usborne Publishing Ltd.,
Usborne House, 83-85 Saffron Hill, London
EC1N 8RT, England.
www.usborne.com

Printed in China.
First published in America in 2005.

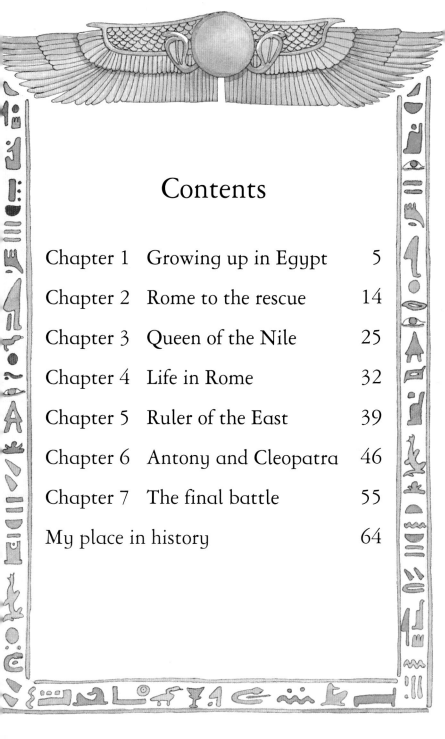

Contents

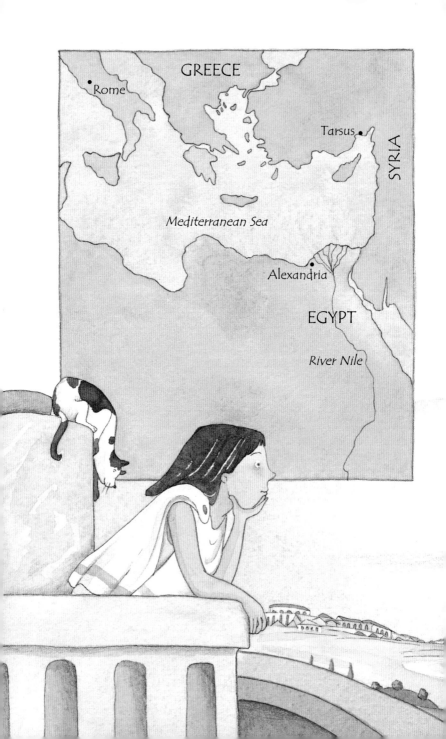

GREECE

Rome

Tarsus

SYRIA

Mediterranean Sea

Alexandria

EGYPT

River Nile

Chapter 1

Growing up in Egypt

From the palace balcony, Princess Cleopatra could see lush gardens reaching down to the sea and a jumble of rooftops stretching far along the coast. Bright sails dotted the shimmering waves, as trade ships came and went with their exotic goods. The Egyptian port of Alexandria was a long way from Greece, the land of her ancestors, but it was the only home Cleopatra knew.

She was imagining herself sailing, the wind against her cheeks, when she heard her Greek nanny calling. "Why can't she leave me in peace?" Cleopatra groaned. But there was still time to hide, so she sped off down a corridor.

Cleopatra had decided to explore every room in her family's palace. This was no small task as there were hundreds of rooms, all gleaming with marble and decorated with exquisite paintings and statues.

By the age of ten, Cleopatra knew the palace inside out. She grew bored of seeing the same faces and longed to learn about new people and places. What happened inside the Egyptian pyramids? Where did the river Nile begin? Why did her Dad go on about Romans all the time?

Every day she pestered her private tutor, who did his best to answer her questions.

Why are all the men in my family called Ptolemy?

It's Greek for "mighty in war" and tells the Egyptians who's boss.

Some answers she found for herself, in the city's huge library.

The Romans rule so many countries!

She learned about the Romans' powerful army and their massive empire that seemed to grow each day.

"It's a good thing Dad has friends in Rome," thought Cleopatra, "or one day the Romans might attack *us*!"

Her family – the Ptolemies – had ruled Egypt for over 250 years and were completely at home in Alexandria. Sometimes, Cleopatra daydreamed about being queen. But, as the third daughter of King Ptolemy XII, she was a long way from the throne. Anyway, she could only ever rule alongside a man. She looked at her baby brother, still gurgling in his cradle. One day he would be King Ptolemy XIII.

Cleopatra was just twelve when she realized her family's reign was in danger. She was reading about Greek

gods, in the shadow of a statue,
when her father walked past
with a nervous minister.

"The Alexandrians are angry that you
owe Rome so much money," said the
minister. "And the Egyptian farmers are
protesting about wheat taxes again."

"They've never liked being ruled by
Greeks," sighed the pharaoh.

"But this time they're planning a
rebellion," the minister went on. "It
might be safest if you went to Rome."

Cleopatra couldn't believe what she'd heard. Her father was the pharaoh – the Egyptians were supposed to treat him as a god. Could he really be under threat?

Something else was worrying her too. Recently, her half-sisters Berenice and little Arsinoe had been whispering together and ganging up against her.

Then, one morning, Cleopatra woke up to shouting. Out of the window, she saw angry Egyptian farmers surrounding the palace.

At breakfast, her sisters looked smug.

"The Egyptians have scared Daddy away," mocked Berenice, making Arsinoe smirk. "Now he'll run to his darling Romans and beg for more help."

Cleopatra was appalled. She'd never liked her sisters much, but how could they be mean about their own father?

It's good that Dad has friends in Rome.

What do *you* know about politics?

The palace felt unsettled without the pharaoh and Cleopatra thought it best to stay out of her sisters' way. She spent her days reading books and teaching herself Egyptian and Latin. As days turned to months, Berenice became more and more bossy and Arsinoe was never far from her side. Even their little brothers, both named Ptolemy, tried to keep their distance.

One day, Berenice called all the servants and family members to a meeting. "From now on, *I* will rule Egypt," she announced.

"But what about Dad?" asked Cleopatra.

"Don't EVER mention his name in my palace again!" Berenice ordered.

Chapter 2

Rome to the rescue

Three years went by without news from Ptolemy XII until, one day, a flurry of excitement swept the palace. An army of soldiers had been spotted entering the city. Cleopatra's father was back... and he had brought support from Rome.

Cleopatra rushed out to welcome her father, but he stormed past her with a fearful scowl on his face.

"Arrest my traitor daughter," he shouted, "then kill her!"

Without hesitation, he had Berenice and her supporters herded together and executed. The message was clear. The pharaoh wouldn't put up with defiance from anyone, especially his own family.

The palace became a gloomy place, where people lived in fear of the pharaoh's wrath. Arsinoe hid in her room, while Cleopatra went back to reading books and keeping a diary. She had plenty to write about. Her father had regained his throne, but the strong presence of the Roman army made him even less popular with the Egyptians.

Now Berenice was dead, Cleopatra was the eldest. But she had stopped dreaming about being queen. It sounded like a nightmare.

Ptolemy XII, with Rome's help, was pharaoh for four more rocky years. As he grew older and weaker, he took more notice of his daughter, who was now an intelligent young woman.

My time as pharaoh is almost over. Be wise and stay close to those with power.

One morning, soon after Cleopatra turned nineteen, her brother burst in to say their father had died.

"That makes me Pharaoh Ptolemy XIII," he boasted.

In tears, Cleopatra vowed to be a worthy daughter. Her father had chosen her to rule Egypt too. The only drawback was that she had to marry her annoying brother, who was only ten years old.

Since the new pharaoh was still a child, he had a group of advisers to help him. Cleopatra didn't trust them. Ambitious, scheming Greeks, led by a crafty man named Pothinus, they wanted to rule Egypt themselves. But Cleopatra was determined to keep her throne.

For three years she fought to stay in control. Her charm and beauty even won over the hearts of the Egyptians, who began to worship her as a goddess. But Cleopatra knew her popularity frustrated Pothinus. When he stopped arguing with her in public, she feared he was plotting something more sinister.

Two days later, there was heavy knocking at her door and ten armed men barged in.

"We have a message for you," said one. "If you're still in Egypt tonight, you're dead!"

Cleopatra fled to Syria, followed by her supporters. While she was massing an army to fight Pothinus, news arrived that the great Roman ruler, Julius Caesar, was in Alexandria.

The Romans helped my father. They might help me too.

Cleopatra decided to set sail for Egypt's capital at once.

She knew she had to arrive in secret, or Pothinus was sure to kill her. So, she waited until dusk, off the coast of Egypt, before sailing to shore.

"Apollodorus!" she called to one of her closest friends. "Come with me... and bring that blanket."

Apollodorus looked Roman, spoke Latin and could easily fool Ptolemy's guards. He and Cleopatra crept ashore and headed for the royal palace.

"Roll me up in your blanket," whispered Cleopatra. "It's the only way I can enter the palace unseen." She kept very still as Apollodorus tucked her under his arm and boldly walked up to the palace gates.

"I have a delivery for Caesar," he told the guards. Then all Cleopatra heard was the sound of heavy footsteps, followed by a loud knock on a door.

"Delivery!" called Apollodorus and Cleopatra tumbled to the floor.

"Who are *you*?" demanded Caesar.

"The Queen of Egypt," replied Cleopatra, in her best Latin, acting as if travel by blanket was normal. Scrambling to her feet, she launched into a speech, explaining her right to the Egyptian throne. Caesar stared in amazement. Women never talked politics to him, but here was someone half his age treating him as an equal.

"I must go," said Cleopatra, at last.

"It's too dangerous," replied Caesar. "Stay here with me."

So she did. It seemed the perfect relationship. Caesar would help Cleopatra win back her throne and, in return, he would have the enchanting Egyptian queen as his ally.

Caesar called a meeting with Pothinus and Ptolemy, and left it with a big smile on his face. "That was easier than I thought," he told Cleopatra. "They've agreed to let you rule again."

"I don't trust them," she replied. "They must be plotting something."

Sure enough, the next day brought trouble. Under Pothinus' orders, soldiers surrounded the palace. Caesar and Cleopatra were trapped.

"Don't worry," whispered Caesar. "My army isn't far away."

Cleopatra could only watch as a bloody battle took place outside the palace. Caesar's men easily squashed Pothinus' soldiers. Even those who escaped the city were trapped by the river Nile.

As the sun set, a centurion arrived at the palace gates. "We've killed Pothinus," he reported to Caesar.

"What about the pharaoh?" asked Cleopatra, hurriedly.

"The boat he was escaping in sank,"

replied the centurion. "We think he's drowned."

Cleopatra panicked. "We must find his body. Immediately!" she told Caesar. He looked confused. "The Nile is sacred to the Egyptian people," Cleopatra explained. "If we don't find my brother, they'll think he was blessed by their gods."

"We can't have that," replied Caesar. "They must believe that *you're* the only one blessed."

After a long search, Caesar's men finally recovered Ptolemy's body. His heavy, gilded uniform had dragged him to the bottom of the river.

Chapter 3

Queen of the Nile

A month later, Cleopatra was enjoying a hot, perfumed bath. It gave her time to relax, before dressing for her next public appearance. She felt safer now that Pothinus and Ptolemy XIII were dead. To become queen again, she'd had to marry her youngest brother – yet another Ptolemy. But at least this one didn't have power-hungry advisers. Besides, with Caesar's love and protection, she could do anything!

Her thoughts were interrupted by Egyptian servants.

"Your Highness," said one, "the priests are expecting you."

Cleopatra let them dress her in rich, golden robes and a heavy black wig. They carefully drew black lines around her eyes, painted her eyelids green and her lips red, then added rouge to her cheeks. The final touch was a golden plumed headdress.

Just then, Caesar came into the room. "You look stunning!" he cried. "That's an impressive headdress."

"These plumes represent Amun Re, king of the gods," explained Cleopatra. "And these two horns are symbols of the goddesses Hathor and Isis."

"No wonder the Egyptians worship you," he replied.

Today, Cleopatra
was leading a procession to
the temple. She made her offerings
and bowed to the priests. They were
powerful men from rich families and
Cleopatra wanted them on her side.
She also wanted their gods' blessings.

But, while the people in Alexandria
adored her, Cleopatra knew she needed
to win over every Egyptian. Otherwise,
they could rise up against her.
Suddenly, she had a brainwave. "I'll
impress them all by taking a grand
trip down the Nile!" she cried.

It was an amazing sight: a luxurious wooden barge, with a gilded bow, billowing sails, sun shades and bright cushions. Cleopatra sat next to Caesar, gazing in wonder as the fertile Egyptian countryside opened out before them. They passed fields and villages, fishermen and crocodiles, pyramids and temples. And, as the dying sun set the river aflame, Cleopatra entertained everyone with music and feasting.

News of Cleopatra's trip journeyed faster than her barge. Farmers and their families gathered on the riverbank to catch a glimpse of their radiant queen. If her barge sailed close to the bank, she would stand up in her flowing robe and regal headdress to talk to the farmers.

The crowds were delighted. None of the other Ptolemies had bothered to leave Alexandria before, let alone learn Egyptian and address the people.

The Nile is the longest river in the world, but for Cleopatra it wasn't long enough. Soon, her barge was heading back to Alexandria. It was like waking up from a wonderful dream.

"I must return to Rome," said Caesar, when they arrived at the palace. "I've been neglecting my duty and my people."

"I'll come with you!" said Cleopatra.

"No," he replied firmly. "The Egyptians need you here to rule them."

"But I need *you*," pleaded Cleopatra.

"All you need is my power," replied Caesar. "I will leave an army of Romans to guard you."

Cleopatra had to watch Caesar go. By now, she was pregnant with his child. When she gave birth to a boy, she knew exactly what to call him.

"He'll be the next Ptolemy to rule Egypt," she thought, "and living proof of Egypt's friendship with Rome. I'll call him Ptolemy Caesar."

Her servants soon nicknamed him Caesarion – little Caesar.

He's got his father's nose.

Chapter 4

Life in Rome

Palace life was dreary without Caesar. Cleopatra adored her son, but a burbling baby wasn't the best company. After many restless nights, she decided to follow Caesar to Rome.

"Pack my belongings," she told her servants. "My son must know his father."

Gossip reached the Egyptian government and one of the ministers dared to question Cleopatra's decision.

"Are you sure it's wise to leave your people?" he ventured.

"The future of Egypt depends on its relationship with Rome," she replied. "I'm going as a duty to my country."

So, Cleopatra and her son set sail for Rome. She took her husband-brother, Ptolemy XIV with her too. He was only a teenager, but she knew he would cause trouble if she left him alone in Egypt.

Cleopatra was confident that Caesar would want to see her, and she wasn't disappointed.

"You'll stay in my villa by the river Tiber and we shall have magnificent parties!" he announced.

The glamorous Roman lifestyle suited Cleopatra perfectly. Every other day seemed to be a festival. She was amazed by the fancy processions, the grand buildings and the lavish banquets.

Meet my dear friend, Antony.

Before long, Cleopatra was hosting her own banquets for Rome's rich and famous. She loved meeting successful people and they were fascinated by her. Everyone wanted to hear about the pyramids, pharaohs and temples of Egypt. She even persuaded some of them to worship her goddess, Isis. But when they asked how she had met Caesar, Cleopatra just smiled.

One early spring evening, Caesar and Cleopatra sat on the balcony, recovering from a seven course meal.

"What's the matter?" Cleopatra asked. "You've been frowning all day."

"There are too many people trying to rule Rome," he said. "We're getting in each other's way and lots of people are insulting me behind my back."

"What Rome needs is a pharaoh!" teased Cleopatra.

"You might be right," replied Caesar, still frowning. "But Rome would never agree."

While Caesar attended meetings,
developed policies and planned battles,
Cleopatra read reports from Egypt. So
far, the Roman troops were keeping the
her people under control. Cleopatra
was delighted. It meant she could stay
in Rome.

But before the trees were in blossom
that year, Cleopatra's peace was
shattered. She was reading a report in
the garden when a messenger arrived,
pale-faced and shaking.

"S-s-s-Caesar's dead!" he stuttered.
"He was st-stabbed at a meeting."

Cleopatra was distraught. She'd grown to love the Roman ruler.

Everyone began discussing who had killed Caesar and why.

Cleopatra had other things on her mind. The people who killed Caesar might come after her and her son. They had to leave Rome.

Chapter 5

Ruler of the East

Cleopatra fled back to Alexandria, with Caesarion and Ptolemy XIV. The young pharaoh had been moody and short-tempered throughout their stay in Rome, but his eyes lit up when he saw his old palace.

Cleopatra was greeted by her ministers. "The people have behaved very well in your absence," they said.

"I'm more worried about my brother, Ptolemy," Cleopatra answered.

The ministers promised to keep a close eye on him. A week later, they announced that Ptolemy had eaten something poisonous and died.

"What a shame," replied Cleopatra, not in the least upset. She immediately had Caesarion crowned pharaoh instead, even though he was only two.

Over the next few years, Cleopatra tried not to think about Rome. She busied herself looking after Egypt. For two years now, the river Nile had failed to flood. The fields were so dry, no crops would grow. Animals were dying and the people were starving.

"It's not your fault if a river doesn't flood," the ministers assured Cleopatra.

"But the Egyptians don't see it that way," she moaned. "They think I'm a goddess with powers over the Nile."

Before long, Cleopatra had more than floods to worry about. A power struggle was taking place in Rome and both sides wanted her help.

First Brutus and Cassius, the men responsible for Caesar's death, sent word to Cleopatra. "Give us ships and soldiers," they wrote, "and we'll protect you and your country."

They're the last people I want to help! But having them as enemies would be even worse...

Within a week, Cleopatra received a similar plea from Antony and Octavian.

Cleopatra was torn. Antony had been one of Caesar's best friends and Octavian was Caesar's adopted son and heir. But if she supported them and they lost, all Egypt would be at the mercy of Brutus and Cassius.

"I must pretend to support both sides," she decided. She wrote to Cassius, explaining that she'd love to help, but the famine in Egypt had weakened her men. Then she wrote to Antony, promising ships... but at the first sign of a storm, she ordered her ships to return home.

In the end, Antony and Octavian were victorious. They divided the Roman empire between them, Octavian taking the west and Antony taking the east. Soon Cleopatra received an angry letter from Antony.

"The Queen of Egypt must come to Tarsus," he wrote, "and explain why she refused to help me."

Tarsus was a city across the Mediterranean sea, where Cleopatra happened to own a palace. She hated being told what to do, but Antony was too powerful to be ignored. She had to appease him somehow... and this time she couldn't arrive in a blanket.

"I'll travel to Tarsus in the royal barge," she told her viziers. "Make sure it's beautifully decorated, lined with the finest silks and covered with gold."

Cleopatra's big dilemma was what to wear. From the tone of his letter, Antony obviously didn't respect her as a queen. She decided to take off her wig and dress up as Aphrodite, the Greek goddess of love and beauty. It was a dramatic gesture, but these were desperate times.

In Tarsus, people flocked to see the famous Egyptian queen for themselves. As Cleopatra's barge glided in to land, the crowds moved aside. There stood Antony, tall and unsmiling. Cleopatra walked bravely up to him. She knew her life depended on this moment.

"You will dine with me tonight," he said.

"No," she replied, in a soft but steady voice. "You will dine with me. I, too, have a palace in Tarsus."

That evening, they feasted like gods. Cleopatra flattered Antony and flirted with him. He would make a very useful ally... and he wasn't bad-looking either.

"Come to Alexandria," she suggested, leading him out onto her terrace. "I'll show you sights you've only ever dreamed of."

"I'd like that," said Antony.

Chapter 6

Antony and Cleopatra

That winter, Antony stayed in Alexandria. Day and night, Cleopatra was at his side. She even accompanied him on hunting trips and watched him exercise his troops.

"A good fighter never turns his back on the enemy," she heard him shout. She couldn't help grinning. This man was celebrated as the best soldier in the Roman empire... and here he was, in Egypt with her!

"I'll make him worship the ground I walk on," she thought. "Then he will only ever fight for *me*."

The two lovers had lots in common. Strong, successful leaders with ambitious plans for the future, they would spend hours discussing how to conquer new lands.

"One day, our Eastern empire will be the richest in the world," Antony would say.

But Antony was married – and his stay in Egypt was cut short when he received worrying news from Fulvia, his wife.

"She's in trouble," he told Cleopatra. "She's been encouraging the Romans to rebel against Octavian."

"I thought you and Octavian were allies," said Cleopatra, confused.

"We were," Antony replied, "but Octavian has decided he wants the Roman empire to himself. Now he's defeated Fulvia and forced her to flee to Greece. I must go and help her rally more support."

Cleopatra hated to think of Antony going back to his wife. But, rather than show her disappointment, she decided to give him a lavish send off. "I'll bewitch him with my charm," she thought. "Then he's sure to come back."

Having concocted the most delicious menu and employed Egypt's top singers and dancers, she dressed once more as

Aphrodite. Antony joined in the fun,
wearing a crown of vine leaves and
pretending to be Aphrodite's lover
– Dionysus, god of wine.

"I'll be back soon," he promised. But
he was away for three and a half years.

In his absence, Cleopatra gave birth
to their twins – Alexander Helios and
Cleopatra Selene.

I wonder if
you'll ever meet
your father.

Once more, Cleopatra put all her energy into ruling Egypt. The country had suffered from bad harvests, but it was still rich, thanks to its large supply of gold. Cleopatra traded gold for food and bought an impressive fleet of ships.

Her spies kept her up-to-date with events in Rome. First, she heard about Fulvia's death. Within weeks, she discovered that Antony had married Octavian's sister, Octavia.

Cleopatra panicked. Her lover had deserted her and made peace with Octavian. Soon, they would want to expand their empire.

"What if they attack Egypt!" Cleopatra gasped. "Who will protect me now?"

But her fears were forgotten when Antony finally returned.

"I've missed my Egyptian beauty," he cried, taking Cleopatra in his arms. When he met his two children, he was overjoyed.

"They're speaking Greek, not Latin," he said. "We'll have to do something about that."

amo...amas... amat...

οὐδὲν λέγει.

To Cleopatra's immense relief, Antony showed no signs of wanting to leave her. He didn't care for Octavian's battle plans and he cared even less for his new wife. But Cleopatra needed to be certain of his loyalty and affection.

"Am I a good queen?" she asked him one afternoon.

"The best in the world!" he replied.

"And do you trust me?" she went on.

"With my own life," he said.

"Then let me buy some countries off you," she said. "I'll pay you in gold..."

"And a hundred kisses," added Antony. It was a deal. Antony needed gold to pay his soldiers and Cleopatra wanted to get back lands to the East that her family had once owned.

Then Antony decided to go one step further to prove his love. He staged a spectacular ceremony where he crowned Cleopatra the Queen of Kings and Caesar's son, Caesarion, the King of Kings. By now, Cleopatra and Antony had three children together and Antony wanted all of them to have royal titles.

Ptolemy Philadephus, I crown you King of Asia Minor.

It was an amazing day for Cleopatra. Crowds of Egyptians gathered to witness the event and celebrate their magical, powerful queen. When Cleopatra saw her children receive their titles, she thought of the glorious futures ahead of them and felt happier than ever.

Chapter 7

The final battle

"I've divorced Octavia," Antony announced to Cleopatra, a year after the crowning ceremony.

"That's fantastic!" said Cleopatra, trying to look pleased, yet worried about Octavian. "But won't her brother get annoyed?"

"It doesn't matter what he thinks," said Antony. "We've got our own empire now. It's none of his business."

Cleopatra fell silent. Throughout her

life, she'd learned to keep Rome on her side in order to remain safe. Now Antony was deliberately cutting all ties with Rome. Surely Octavian would come after him.

Cleopatra readied her ships to fight the Romans if necessary and encouraged Antony to assemble an army. Many Egyptians were eager to fight for their queen and Antony still had a loyal following of Roman soldiers.

Before long, a messenger arrived with news from Rome. Octavian had publicly declared war, not against Antony... but against Cleopatra.

"I won't let him attack Egypt," said Cleopatra, fiercely. "If he wants a battle, I'll take my warships to Greece and fight him there."

"We'll go together," said Antony. "Once we've defeated Octavian, we can sail on to Rome for a victor's welcome."

All winter they waited in Greece for Octavian to attack. But it wasn't until spring that his fleet finally arrived – and it was much larger than Cleopatra and Antony expected.

"We're trapped!" announced Ahenobarbus, one of Antony's advisers. "Octavian has positioned his troops to the north and has sent his admiral, Agrippa, to block off the port."

"We must march overland to fight Octavian," said Crassus, Antony's military commander.

"And leave my ships?" cried Cleopatra. "Never! My treasure is stored on board. If we lose it, we'll never be able to buy a new fleet."

By morning, the situation was worse. A group of soldiers, including Ahenobarbus, had deserted.

"The traitors have run to Octavian," fumed Antony. "You're right, Cleopatra. We must protect our ships and fight Octavian another day."

As they left the port, Agrippa's fleet attacked them. Cleopatra's ship was the fastest and managed to escape with the treasure. She looked back through the chaos of the battle. Where was Antony? Eventually his ship caught up with hers but his expression was glum. They had lost many ships and even more men.

Antony sulked for weeks but Cleopatra went straight back to work. She used some of the treasure to restore her fleet of ships. Then she stored the rest in a magnificent tomb that was being built for her. "When I die," she thought, "this tomb will be a glorious gateway to the afterlife."

Meanwhile, Octavian was advancing on Egypt and many of Antony's men were giving themselves up rather than fighting back. Cleopatra summoned a messenger. "Tell Octavian that I'll give up my throne," she said, "if he'll let my children rule instead of me."

She never received an answer.

"Octavian's army has reached Alexandria," announced Antony the next day. "I'll ride out to attack him." He embraced Cleopatra and left.

Cleopatra called for three faithful servants. "Let's go to my tomb," she said. "We'll be safe there and we can protect Egypt's treasure from Octavian."

From the tomb's window, Cleopatra kept watch. Soon, a messenger arrived. "Antony has stabbed himself!" he cried. "He heard you were in your tomb and thought you'd been killed!"

"That can't be true!" wailed Cleopatra. "Bring him here."

When Antony arrived, he was soaked in blood and could hardly talk. Cleopatra took him in her arms.

As Antony drew his last breath, Octavian's soldiers charged into the monument. They had conquered Alexandria and now they wanted Cleopatra as their prize. "This will be your prison," they shouted, "until we take you back to Rome."

Cleopatra's face gave away no emotion, but inside she knew her world had ended. Antony was dead, she had lost her throne and she could no longer protect her beloved children.

"I refuse to be Octavian's victory trophy," she thought. Quickly, she wrote a letter and asked a soldier to deliver it to his general. Then she whispered something to a servant.

"May I fetch my mistress some fruit?" asked the servant.

"I guess so," replied a soldier.

Within an hour, the servant was back with a basket of figs. Cleopatra, now dressed in golden robes, lifted each fig until she found what she was looking for – a poisonous snake. Holding the snake to her arm, she let it prick her skin with its deadly fangs.

By the time Octavian received her letter, Cleopatra was dead. The letter was her final request – to be buried alongside her beloved Antony.

7o BC – I was born in Alexandria, Egypt.

58 BC – My Dad, Ptolemy XII, flees to Rome. My horrible half-sister, Berenice, steals the throne.

55 BC – Dad kills Berenice and reclaims the throne.

51 BC – Dad dies and I become queen (with my annoying little brother, Ptolemy XIII).

47 BC – I meet Caesar. He tries to bring peace to Egypt but Ptolemy and his evil adviser, Pothinus, attack us. Both of them are killed in battle. Caesar and I travel in style down the Nile.

46 BC – I spend a fantastic year in Rome.

44 BC – Caesar is murdered and I return to Egypt.

41 BC – I meet Antony in Tarsus.

34 BC – Antony crowns me Queen of Kings and my children all receive royal titles.

32 BC – Octavian rudely declares war on me.

31 BC – Octavian traps me and Antony at a port in Greece. We escape with our treasure.

3o BC – Octavian's troops reach Alexandria. Antony kills himself, thinking I'm dead. I decide to kill myself too, so Octavian can't gloat over me in Rome.

* * *

P.S. Did you wonder what happened to:

Arsinoe? She turned against Cleopatra, was captured by Caesar and later executed by Antony.

Cleopatra's children? Caesarion was murdered and the other three were sent to live with Octavia in Rome. Cleopatra Selene went on to marry an African king.